# SIX FIGURE AUTHOR

## USING DATA TO SELL BOOKS

CHRIS FOX

*For Tammi.*
*We're a hell of a team.*

# CONTENTS

**WRITE FASTER, WRITE SMARTER SERIES**

5,000 Words Per Hour
Lifelong Writing Habit
Write to Market
Launch to Market
Six Figure Author
Relaunch Your Novel

# INTRODUCTION

Wow, that's some cover, huh? I've got the click-bait title, with a gigantic pile of cash underneath. It's like the punchline to an internet marketing joke, right? Here's the thing: It's absolutely accurate. I make six figures selling books. More importantly, I make six figures selling *fiction*. Nor am I the only author I know doing so. There are dozens of us, and my goal with this book is to teach you to do the same thing.

To do that, you're going to need to approach publishing differently than nearly every author out there. If you want to make six figures writing books, you need to sell books like it's 2017—not like it's 1999. Unfortunately, most of us are taught to do exactly that. A great deal of the marketing advice floating around is dated, and wasn't terribly effective to begin with.

So what will this book do that others haven't? I'm going to teach you how Amazon uses data to sell books (and a host of other products). You'll learn how you can tap into the multi-billion-dollar sales engine they've created. In fact, you'll learn why they *want* you to do exactly that.

What you'll learn may not gel immediately. It requires some counterintuitive thinking, especially if you've been steeped in the "sell as many books as possible" mantra. It isn't about *how many* copies you sell. It's *who* you sell those copies to.

We're two hundred words into this book, and that's as many as I'm willing to waste on "what this book will teach you." Let's dive right in.

Before we do that, I know some of you want a little more information about the author, so you'll find that below. I can sum it up for you if you want to skip to chapter one: *Blah, blah, blah, I'm a big deal, blah, blah, sell lots of books, blah, data science.*

## ABOUT THE AUTHOR

If you've read any of my other books for writers, you already know who I am. If not, here's the skinny:

I published my first novel in October of 2014. Since then, I've sold over a hundred thousand books, and had nearly ten million page reads in Kindle Unlimited. I write science fiction, post-apocalyptic fiction, and books for writers. As of this writing, I have fourteen books in print.

What makes me a little different from other successful writers is that I've put my entire career under a microscope. Since day one I've documented my experiments (like the 21 Day Novel Writing Challenge), and writers have followed along. Some have been with me since the first month. They watched me go from my first sale to quitting my lucrative mobile app developer job so I could write full time.

That developer job is the real reason you're holding this book. Now more than ever, selling books is more about technology than publishing. The world has changed, and we need to change with it. Fortunately for me, I worked at a San Francisco startup at exactly the right time. I was in the beating heart of the tech world at the exact moment modern indie publishing was born.

What many people don't realize is that every startup, from Facebook to LinkedIn to Uber to Fitbit, is within a few miles of the others. They're in the financial district of San Francisco, the real tech hub of the world. Silicon Valley is old news.

Until recently, I worked for a startup called Cell-Scope. At that startup, I learned all about data science and machine learning. I worked alongside people with PhDs from Stanford, Berkeley, and Harvard. They were some of the best in the world at what they did, and what they did was invent the future. I learned how Facebook uses facial recognition, and how Netflix knows which shows you're likely to binge-watch.

More importantly, **I learned how Amazon sells products**. Amazon has an office in San Francisco, and the developer community is very close knit. Every year Amazon hosted a tech conference just a couple blocks from my office, and I spent time hanging out with their engineers. Like all engineers, we enjoyed talking about our latest creations, and *their* latest creations were the methodologies being used to sell products...like our books.

I leveraged the hell out of that opportunity. In February of this year I gave up my six-figure startup job (no, I will not be writing *Six Figure Engineer*), and became a full-time author. Since then, I've gone on to make more money than I ever did at CellScope. Books are more lucrative than software, if you approach this business correctly.

I've already eclipsed my developer salary for the year, and I'm writing this in September. It is my sincere hope that reading this book helps you to do exactly the same thing.


-Chris

*For more information:*
www.chrisfoxwrites.com

## 1

## IS SIX FIGURES REALLY ACHIEVABLE?

"Six Figure Author" is a bold claim. Can *you* really make six figures selling books? More to the point, can you do it selling fiction, instead of peddling how-to books to authors?

The short answer is *yes*, but it will take an immense amount of the *right kind* of work. The long answer is the rest of this book. It offers a blueprint, a way to generate five figures a month selling books in popular genres.

How do I know that blueprint works? Not because I've used it myself, though I've had more than one $20,000 month. I know it works because I've seen dozens of authors use the exact same blueprint, with very similar results. I've watched as people whose book sales wouldn't pay for a night out suddenly started pulling in four-figure days. The things they've done, you can do, too.

I'm not talking about outliers, either. You don't need to be Andy Weir or Hugh Howey to make a great living at this; quite the opposite. People like you and I won't become household names, but we can make a wonderful living selling books. It's *those* authors I chose as case studies for this book.

Every last one that broke out of the pack has one thing in common: we all identified our audience with laser precision. We knew who'd be interested in our books, before we published the book. This book will teach you how to use that as the foundation for a beautiful career.

If you've read *Write to Market*, you already know how to write a book that a large audience will love. *Six Figure Author* takes it to the next level. We dive into the piece that separates those authors who are struggling from those who've made it to that six-figure promised land.

## A Sale Is Never Just a Sale

Tell me if this sounds familiar:

You launched your first book. In between

refreshing the KDP dashboard to check sales, you logged in to Twitter, Facebook, and any other social media you use. You told the world about your book. You even emailed your uncle Carl, whom you only see at Easter. You put out the word, and your family and friends responded.

You sold a couple hundred books, yay! There were even a few reviews. But sales flatlined, and never came back. You've tried advertising, you've run promotions. But nothing works long-term. The book just refuses to keep selling, and you're starting to despair. Maybe you wrote a second book, and a third. Maybe a tenth. Each one has had similar results, and you just can't seem to break out.

Meanwhile, some wide-eyed new author breezes onto the scene and their debut novel sells like gang-busters. So what did they do differently? By chance or design, that author's book landed squarely in front of a large target audience, one predisposed to buy books like that one.

Unfortunately for us, when we sold books to everyone we knew, we polluted our data. Amazon wasn't able to identify our audience, which is why our book didn't take off. We'll get into the specifics of how and why that happens, but for now focus on this: **a sale isn't just a sale.** How many books you sell at launch isn't nearly as important as **who you sell them to.**

When your mom and your work friend and your husband all bought a copy of your book, Amazon took notes. Amazon was trying to figure out what those people had in common. Unfortunately, the thing those people have in common is *you*. Not their love of whatever the heck you write.

That matters more than you might think. In the modern age, books are sold with data science, and that becomes more true every day. Gone are the days of shotgun advertising. Everything is carefully targeted. Authors who understand that are making their fortunes. Six figures is within your grasp, if you can learn to target the right audience. Hell, I know at least three authors you've never heard of that have had six-figure *months*.

Sounds great, right? What's the catch?

## Remember That Work I Mentioned?

If you've read my other books you already know what I'm going to say. Nothing you read here will be useful unless you **do the work.** Above, I said that I know dozens of authors who are making six figures.

That may sound like a lot, but consider this. I've sold thousands of copies of *Write to Market*, but only a few dozen authors have done anything with the material. Why? Because writing to market is hard work, especially if you put out books quickly (and you need to).

Many people gave up. They gave writing to market a try, but found it too overwhelming. Don't be that person. Be one of the few dozen who persevered. Do the work, because you want the rewards.

That work starts here, by reading this book. At the end of every chapter you're going to see an exercise. I wrote that exercise for a reason. Each one is designed to get you to practice one of the fundamentals of selling your book. The skills you learn doing this will be necessary as your career progresses. **Do. The. Exercises.**

If you are like me and prefer to read the book straight through first, that's cool. You'll find the exercises compiled into an appendix at the end. But if you do read straight through, make sure you sit down at the end and do those exercises. If you don't, I'll call your mother and tell her. Seriously. Okay, not seriously.

## 2

## HOW AMAZON SELLS BOOKS

It's time for the nitty gritty. If you want to sell a huge pile of books, then you need to understand how books are sold today. Not how they were sold in the 90s. Not how they were sold even three years ago. *Today*. Right now.

More specifically, you need to understand how books are sold on Amazon. Why? Why not Apple or Google or Kobo, or some aggregate of all of them? The answer comes down to *how* Amazon sells books —how, in fact, they sell everything.

Amazon's core business is not retail. They are *not* just an online store. They are a data-driven company, a buzzword borrowed from my time in the startup world. Data-driven simply means that Amazon is in business to build a better sales engine, not to sell more products. The more efficient they get at automating the process of selling, the more profitable they become. In the next chapter we'll get into the nuts and bolts of machine learning. In this chapter, we're going to explain how Amazon is using it.

## How Apple, Google, and Nook Sell Books

In April of 2015 I removed my books from Amazon's Kindle Unlimited program. Doing so allowed me to list them on other retailers, and the one that most excited me was Apple. They'd approached me, convincing me that I'd sell enough books with them to make up for anything lost from Kindle Unlimited.

Working with the iBooks team was amazing, and I even had the chance to join them for lunch at their Cupertino campus. The iBooks team were true to their word. They set up promotions for my books, including a gigantic banner on the front page of the Science Fiction & Fantasy section of iTunes. I was thrilled, especially when the sales numbers came in. I cannot say enough good things about working with Apple.

Unfortunately, after the promotions ended, my sales flatlined. The only sales I saw could be traced back to my own efforts. After talking with many friends in the same genre, I realized they were all having the same problem. Apple sales were great at launch, but stagnated quickly.

This intrigued me, being the data geek that I am. So I began to study Apple. I talked to engineer friends who worked there, asking their opinions. In the end it confirmed what I believed: **Apple is 100% a boutique retailer**, meaning that a human chooses which books to promote. Without that, there was no organic discovery tool where readers could find your book. Remember this when you read how Amazon sells books.

As for Kobo, Nook, and Google Play, I never had enough sales to study how their ecosystems worked. I know authors who've done very well at all of them, but I can't comment from direct experience. What I can say is that everything I made from those retailers over the course of a year would barely buy a steak dinner.

Needless to say, I moved my books back into Kindle Unlimited in April of 2016. The instant I did that I began making more money. Here's why.


**How Amazon Sells Books**

Amazon's approach to selling books is radically different than the rest of the industry's. It's this, more than anything else, that makes them so vital to becoming a six-figure author. So what are they doing that's so revolutionary?

Amazon is, effectively, building an artificial intelligence capable of determining what you will buy. They've been using machine learning for over a decade, and the sole purpose is to figure out your habits. They've logged everything you've ever bought, and in my case this data goes back to 2002. They know that I purchased *Lord of the Rings*, so I'd want the new *Hobbit* movies. I like Brandon Sanderson, so Amazon pointed me at Patrick Rothfuss.

They know how many books I bought in 2015, versus 2012. They know which authors caused me to buy my way through their entire series (I bought all sixteen in the Dresden Files). This data is extremely valuable both to Amazon and to us, especially when you begin applying machine learning.

Amazon employs hundreds of data scientists, and many more software engineers. Their entire job is to make the sales engine more accurate. They are succeeding spectacularly at this, especially in the last twelve months. Amazon's reach is global, and they have over two hundred million accounts.

Amazon knows a lot more than we give them credit for.

The most visible way you see this at play is the "Also Bought" items on your Amazon product page. It's become conventional wisdom that smart authors want to see books very similar to their own in that area. It's wisdom I subscribe to, especially since I understand why Amazon has linked those particular books together.

Once those links are forged, Amazon will use them to put your book in front of people they think likely to buy it. This comes largely in one of two ways. Either they send out an email to a highly targeted group they feel may like your book, or they show your book to select customers directly on their home page. They do this under "Recommended for You," and you'll see it every time you visit their site.

Those recommendations are the result of highly refined machine learning. What *you* see is very different from what I, or anyone else, would see. The recommendations are affected by our geographic location, our age, and our purchase history. They'll be affected by other internet searches we've run that have nothing to do with Amazon, because Amazon's reach is vast.

Affiliate sites often include a tracking pixel,

which means any site you visit could be transmitting your identity right back to Amazon. This tells Amazon even more about you, and when it begins creepily recommending wedding stuff to you that's why. Amazon knows you were visiting bridal sites.

## How This Impacts You

Amazon wants to sell as much stuff as possible. Above all, they value the customer. Not you—you're a supplier. Your needs are secondary. Amazon only cares about the customer, as well they should. Understanding that fact will help you and Amazon work together to sell books.

Since we know that Amazon has the power to show your book to tons of readers, working with them is just smart business. The more efficiently you can do that, the more books you will sell.

Remember that bit in the last chapter about a sale never being just a sale? Here's the why: If you can show Amazon the exact type of person who will love your book, then they'll be able to show it to a whole bunch of those people. **If you can give Amazon several hundred sales to a highly targeted audience, then Amazon will**

**quickly and easily go find more people just like them.**

This is why I push hard at the launch of a new book, but then put it on autopilot. Once I've fed Amazon the correct data, they know how to sell my book far better than I ever will. And they sell a whole lot of copies on my behalf. No other retailer in the world does this, which is why I've become such a big fan of Amazon. I like my five-figure months, and those only started happening once I learned how to use the tools Amazon has created.

## Does This Mean Being Exclusive With Amazon?

I want to address this now, because it's a divisive topic in the author community. Some people believe you should be exclusive with Amazon, others feel that putting all their eggs in one basket is too risky. Where do I come down? Put all your eggs in the basket. Then go get some more eggs, and put them in, too. You want your entire new release portfolio listed in Kindle Unlimited.

That's a bold recommendation, I know. What happens if Amazon cuts your royalties in half tomorrow? They could. Or they could simply ban your account in a freak twist, and where would that leave you? There's no doubt that being reliant on one company is scary.

I do it anyway. I do it because I make far, far more money that way. During an interview on the Science Fiction & Fantasy Marketing podcast, Nick Webb was asked why he used Kindle Unlimited. He pointed out that Amazon is the largest bookstore in the world. The second largest is Kindle Unlimited. He's 100% right about that. My page reads generate thousands of dollars a month, eclipsing all other retailers combined.

The thing is, the extra money isn't even the reason I stay in Kindle Unlimited (though, let's be real: the money is nice). The real reason to stay is *data*. Kindle Unlimited is full of voracious readers—I call them serial readers. These serial readers are the topic of an entire chapter in this book, because they are absolutely vital to your long term success. If you can find a few hundred, you have enough to train Amazon. With those readers you can almost guarantee that it will sell the heck out of your books.

This will also trigger a snowball effect. Kindle Unlimited borrows count as sales, which moves your book up in rank. As your book rises in rank, more people see it. Some of those people will buy it; some will borrow it. The combination is what will cause your book to break into the Amazon top #1,000, and has led to *four figure days* for me. In one case I had seven of them in a row, earning $10,000 in a week. The really funny thing? I know authors who'd cry if they had my numbers, because that would be *low* for them.

Here's the bottom line: If you want your new release to blow up, you need Kindle Unlimited to make that happen. You don't have to trust me on that, either. The exercise below is where I start proving that what I'm saying is true. You're going to see how Amazon differs from the other retailers, because you're going to test it yourself.

**Exercise #1-** Fire up Amazon's home page. Mouse over your account button and click on "Your Recommendations." You'll see a bunch of categories, each showing what Amazon thinks you're interested in.

Now run five searches for books in a genre you don't normally read. If nothing leaps to mind, just look up "Chris Fox." Click each of the books you searched for.

Go back to Your Recommendations. If the books

you searched for were in a new category, it should now appear. In my case, I searched for Western Novels and clicked the first five books in the search. All of a sudden, Historical Books showed up in my recommendations. Creepy, right? That's the power of data science.

**Bonus**- Go to iTunes, Barnes & Noble, or Google Play. Repeat this exercise. Note that nothing visible changes. Only Amazon is reacting to immediate changes in data. The rest of the retailers are light years behind.

## 3

## WTF IS DATA SCIENCE?

T hroughout this book you're going to hear terms like "data science," "neural networks," and "machine learning." You've already heard at least a couple, and might have no clue what they are. This chapter breaks them down in layman's terms.

It's critical that you understand at least the basics of each, because these concepts govern our modern world. That will be even more true in five years— and in ten, every facet of our life will be affected.

Almost every major corporation is already capitalizing on data science. Even the publishing house Simon & Schuster, famous for being slow to adapt, finally hired their first data scientist. They know it's the future, and they're scared of the power it gives indie authors like us. We can find our audiences directly, without needing a middleman.

## What Is Data Science?

My first brush with data science came in 2012, not long after I took a job at CellScope. We hired a guy affectionately known as "Doctor Dan." Dan was a data scientist with a doctorate from Stanford, and also one of the most brilliant people I'd ever met. If you've ever seen the show *The Big Bang Theory*, think of a very athletic Sheldon who likes to run triathlons. That was Dan.

When Dan started at CellScope I asked him what he did. He gave me a complex answer about patterns and neural networks. It was completely unhelpful, but over the next several months I learned what he was talking about. **Data science uses large amounts of data to see patterns that wouldn't otherwise be clear**.

One of the most common examples of data science is facial recognition. When you upload a photo to Facebook, how does Facebook know where the face is? How does it instantly know how many faces there are, and in many cases know which of your friends are in the picture?

That's data science. This particular example uses a blend of image processing and machine learning. Let me explain.

## Machine Learning

Machine learning is exactly what it sounds like: building machines that can learn. Data scientists use computer programming to write baby artificial intelligences. These intelligences are usually called classifiers, and use a "brain" called a neural network to learn about whatever the programmer has designed them to master.

In the case of Facebook, their facial recognition AI knows all about faces. Their programmers created a definition for nose, ears, eyes, chin, eyebrows, mouth, and probably two or three dozen other features.

Once these definitions had been created, they fed their baby AI hundreds of thousands of images. Each image contained a face, with a helpful little line drawn around every feature. Facebook's AI digested all of these.

The programmers taught this AI that if enough of these things were present in an image, then it was a face. This process is called **training**. Facebook used machine learning to train their AI, and that's why they can tag faces with almost 100% accuracy.

At CellScope, we used machine learning to identify the human eardrum, and to figure out whether or not you had an ear infection. I saw these concepts applied in real time, and even taught our baby AI to know when our microscope was attached to your cell phone.

Machine learning is a broad field, and can be used for all sorts of things. You see it in almost every aspect of your life, and the number of uses grows every year. Recently, Google even digested 11,000 novels to teach its AI to write better sentences.

Interesting stuff, but the most important use, for our purposes, is selling books.


## Tying Data Science Back to Amazon

So we now know that data science and machine learning require large amounts of data, and data scientists to manipulate that data. Guess who has both a massive amount of user data, and a huge team of data scientists to utilize it? You guessed it: Amazon. Many of us forget how long they've been around, or that there was a ever time you'd buy things in—*gasp*—an actual store.

Amazon as we know it first came online in 1995. For the first six years they lost money, but their shareholders seemed unconcerned. Every year they lost a little less, and in 2001 they finally made their first profit. What kind of nutjob creates an online company that loses money for 6 years?

The kind that sees where the future is going. Amazon will be one of the first true artificial intelligences, just like you've seen in movies like 2001 and Terminator. Everything they've done since they first launched has been to create an **artificial intelligence** capable of **understanding what every person in the world is going to buy.**

They've been quietly studying you, me, everyone. They study China, Australia, and every other nation where people use their service. That massive quantity of data allows them to understand buying patterns in ways that are nearly impossible for the average person to understand. Amazon has dozens of the top data scientists in the world, each working to refine their baby artificial intelligence. Every day they come up with new experiments, and they're continuously modifying how they sell products.

You already know the bottom line. Amazon can find customers for just about anything. They can do this with a frightening degree of accuracy, and every day they get better at it. This Orwellian stuff is great news for authors. Why? Because you now understand that Amazon is powered by data. If you can supply them the right kind of data, then Amazon will happily deliver thousands—or even tens of thousands—of sales.

**Exercise #2-** This exercise won't teach you to sell books, but it will show you a simple, practical application for data science. Copy a chapter from your latest work in progress, then go to Wordclouds.com. Click the file button, which will open a menu. Select paste, and paste in the chapter you copied.

Look at the resulting word cloud. Notice words that appear frequently are larger. I use this technique to identify words that I tend to over use. Never again will I use *acrid* 23 times in a single novel.

**Bonus:** Use this process for your entire novel, and eliminate any words you see yourself overusing.

## 4

# THE POWER OF DATA

D ata science sounds cool and all, but the six-figure question is still looming: How do you get Amazon to sell books on your behalf?

You do it by training Amazon's classifiers. Just like Facebook used hundreds of thousands of faces to teach their AI to identify them, you're going to teach Amazon to identify your target reader. That does require a few hundred well-targeted sales.

If that sounds daunting, don't worry. Much of the rest of this book will teach you to identify your target audience. For now, let's focus on **purity of data.** That concept is huge, and will mean the difference between Amazon selling thousands of books, or giving up on your book.

Remember that every sale is a customer profile,

and as they accumulate, Amazon starts comparing them to identify which purchases they have in common. If you're pretty sure that readers of Nick Webb, Joshua Dalzelle, and Richard Fox will love your book, then all you have to do is find readers who bought from all three authors.

There are several chapters to help do that, but before we can start zeroing in on our audience we need to understand how Amazon will use the data we provide.

## How Does Amazon Use Data?

It's important to realize that Amazon tracks a lot more than which other products people have purchased. There's a lot more going on under the hood, especially where books are concerned.

Amazon tracks every click on their website. When you first log in a session is created, and every time you come back to Amazon.com you start another one. During these sessions, Amazon is measuring everything they can. They know every last thing you've ever searched for, even the misspelled things. They know which products you bought, but more importantly they also know which ones you didn't. This allows them to calculate any given product's **conversion rate**.

Conversion rate is simply the percentage of people who buy your product after visiting the product page. Now that I've published so many books I've had a chance to see this in action, both for books that sell, and books that fail to. I finally understand exactly how conversion rate influences the actions Amazon is willing to take on my behalf.

By the time I launched *Hero Born*, in December of 2015, I had a decent-sized platform. I was able to get thousands of eyes on the book, but my conversion rate was low. Most people who visited the product page didn't buy. Because of this, even though I had a good number of sales, the book tanked. Amazon did almost no promotion on my behalf, so once I'd exhausted my own avenues, *Hero Born* lost all momentum.

Contrast this with *Destroyer*. That book had a very high conversion ratio. A lot of the people who visited the page bought it. Amazon sat up and took notice. When they see a product with a high conversion rate, they put it in front of more people. If a lot of those people convert, Amazon keeps putting your book in front of *more* people. Upping your conversion rate is the fastest and best way to get Amazon to sell for you.

Conversion rate isn't black-and-white, though. Amazon uses all that fancy data science to figure out **who converted.** *Which people* who visited your book page bought the book? What else have they bought? What are the similarities between those products? Are there are other Amazon users who have those similarities, and might buy your new book? Amazon can calculate the answer instantly.

Amazon knows you binge-read mysteries. They know you do it most often on Sundays, which is why you often buy books before bed on Saturday evening. If you read the book in their Kindle App, they know how much of it you read the first day. They know you devour some books, but never make it past 20% on others.

They have this information about everyone who has ever bought any book through KDP. They have oceans of data at their disposal, and they're using this data to get more accurate at predicting who will buy what. They have a vested interest in putting your book in front of every last person who might buy it, but they don't like showing people things they aren't interested in.

If your conversion rate is low, Amazon figures

that their customers aren't interested, so they stop showing your book. If your conversion rate is high enough, though, Amazon can propel you to stardom.

Ever heard of Andy Weir and his book *The Martian*? That book was indie published, first in a serialized format on Weir's website, then later as an ebook on Amazon. By the time it was listed as an ebook, thousands of science fiction fans were ready to buy. They'd followed Andy's work for years, and wanted to support him.

Since those fans shared similar interests, Amazon's algorithms knew instantly who to show the book to. It happily peddled *The Martian* to science fiction fans, and those fans converted in droves. Amazon showed it to more people, and *those* people bought it in droves. So Amazon showed it to even more people. The audio book release just threw gasoline on the fire.

When all was said and done, Weir had sold a half million copies, long before he had a movie deal or a traditional publishing deal. Andy didn't spend a dime on advertising. His success is one hundred percent driven by data science. Let that sink in. Andy Weir is a seven-figure author created entirely by Amazon.

We don't have to be anywhere near his league to make a very comfortable six-figure living.

**Exercise #3-** How long have you had your Amazon account? Go to your purchase history, all the way back to the beginning...as far as it will let you. What was the first thing you bought? What are all the things you've bought since then? Spend a little time browsing. What do you think these things say about you to Amazon? How is Amazon using that data?

**Bonus:** Pick two years: the first year you had your Amazon account, and this year. How many books did you buy in each year? Has it gone up or down? Why?

## 5

# FINDING YOUR TARGET AUDIENCE

I f you want to get Amazon to peddle your book, you need a few hundred sales to a target audience. But how do you get your target audience? How do you begin to understand who they are, and what they want? That sounds like a monumental task, and it is. It's not something you're going to learn instantly, and it is going to require a lot of diligent experimentation on your part.

This is at once both easier and harder than you'd expect. Easier, because there's a series of steps you can follow to do it. Harder, because those steps take time, research, and often a thick skin. Most books sugar-coat the truth, and tell you getting rich is as easy as this:

1. Run some Facebook ads
2. ???
3. Profit

It isn't that simple, and some part of all of us senses that. Learning about the community of people who will buy your books is a big investment. Locating them is just the first step. After that, before you can even tell them about your book, you need to join the tribe. It's a process, but the rewards are well worth it.

## Where Do You Start?

No matter what you write, there is something similar out there. Even your genre-bending novel meets a specific set of **reader expectations**. People pick it up for a reason, and the kind of enjoyment they get is the same kind they'll get from similar books.

You need to locate those other books. You need to understand who writes fiction similar to you—and when I say "who," I mean authors who are selling a ton of books. Not the household names, like Gaiman or Patterson, but the midlisters whose books are regularly breaking into the top #1,000.

Authors like James Patterson are simply too large

to target. People read their books because of the author's brand, not because of genre. I've read every book Brandon Sanderson has written, and he spans YA, epic fantasy, and western-themed fantasy. This means that, even though I might have a book similar to one of his, I can't use him for direct comparison.

I need to find authors who are only known for the genre I want to write in. Those of you who picked up *Write to Market* or *Launch to Market* know that I chose Nick Webb to study. He had exactly the kind of success I was after in Military Science Fiction, but he's not nearly as famous as David Webber. That made Nick the perfect place to research my target audience.

You need to find your equivalent authors, the people selling *today*. I realize this can be a little daunting, especially if you haven't even finished writing your first book. But if I could go back two years and tell myself one thing, this would be it: Find other authors like me before doing anything else.

## How Do I Know Which Authors Are Like Me?

This is one of the pieces that will separate the dozens who become six-figure authors from the thousands who do not. If you want to know who writes like you, then you need to **read other authors** —a lot of other authors. You need to go through the same discovery process your target reader does. That means showing up to Amazon and browsing the categories where you think your book will fit.

Buy several of the top books in that category, and read them. Do you enjoy them? Do they feel at least somewhat similar to what you write? Would the people who read them be interested in your book as well? This can be difficult to determine, but fortunately there's a way to find out. In *Write to Market* we spent time reading the reviews for the top books in a given genre, and we're going to do that here, too.

You can learn a great deal about reader expectations from reading reviews. Both the one-star and five-star reviews will tell you a lot about what those people like and dislike. If a lot of reviews complain about a book not getting the science right, and you know that your book *does* get the science right, then it will meet that particular reader expectation.

**Destroyer Case Study**

Let's take a look at a real world example. We'll use

*Destroyer*, since it's already familiar (and lets me promote my own book, *muhaha*). As of this writing, *Destroyer* has 250 reviews. Its average score is 4.6, and here is the top positive review:

*5.0 out of 5 stars*

**Battlestar Galactica Meets Mass Effect Describes It Perfectly**

If you are a reader of space action novels, shorter space opera, or plot-driven military SF, you will enjoy this book.

"Destroyer" doesn't try to reinvent the wheel of fast-paced science fiction. It doesn't break new ground or knock you off your feet. But it DOES keep you engaged from start to finish. The storyline will be familiar to readers of this genre, but the journey is fun all the same.

In short, the book starts off with a bang, jumping into action pretty quick. After some fighting (no spoilers), the middle of the book centers around the mystery of who attacked the Tigris science vessel and who is destroying all these colonies. The villainous species is an interesting, if not wholly original, take on homicidal aliens mixed with artificial intelligence.

All in all, the book's main weakness is also its greatest strength: it sticks very close to the subgenre's tropes. It's got all the elements you'd expect, and yet it's an enjoyable and interesting ride to the end.

Here is the top negative review:

*2.0 out of 5 stars*

**Terrible science. Mediocre plot.**

Somewhat interesting plot, but TERRIBLE science. The galaxy rotates every 26,000 years? No, more like every 250,000,000 years where our sun is, and the rotation is totally different at different points from the center. Uranium has 235 protons in it's nucleus? No - it has 92. 235 is the atomic weight (protons plus neutrons) of one

Uranium isotope. "Helios gates"? Absurd - nothing could possibly allow starships to dive into stars to reach warp gates at the very center. I gave up about 30% of the way through. Lots better military sci-fi out there.

*Destroyer* doesn't break any new ground, and most readers are fine with that, hence the 4.6 average. It's run-of-the-mill science fiction that long-time readers are very familiar with. The book's scientific research was non-existent, and those readers who are expecting their science to make sense will be (loudly) disappointed.

Thankfully, those scientific sticklers were in the minority. Most people in this genre were happy with a fun space romp, and didn't look too closely at the physics holding the universe together.

If you are also writing military science fiction, you'll need to take a very close look at your book. How much time and attention are you giving to the science? If the answer is "a ton," then *Destroyer* is not a good book for you to compare with.

You'll want to find other books where the reviews

mentioned how much they loved the hard science. Then you'd want to study those authors, because their books are more similar to yours. The differences are small, but extremely important. Both *Destroyer* and *The Expanse* are about spaceships and aliens, but the approach each takes is radically different.

My readers want action. Most hated *The Expanse*. *The Expanse* readers want realistic science, and an immersive experience. Their eye would twitch every third page when they read the implausible science in *Destroyer*. See the difference?

We need to find our exact audience. Just liking science fiction isn't enough. We need to find the people who will enjoy our books because they appreciate our strengths, and it takes a lot of diligent reading to understand who these people are and where these people can be found.

Your character-driven space opera has an audience, but you aren't going to find it by marketing to people who read *Destroyer*. They want action, first and foremost. So if that's you—if you find that your book doesn't match the author you checked out— what do you do? You keep reading. You keep looking at other authors, until you find something that more closely resembles your book. If you wrote a character-driven space opera, you keep reading until you find Lindsay Buroker's *Star Nomad.* It has action, sure. But the character development is much more pronounced than in *Destroyer.*

*Star Nomad*'s reviews back up that assertion. Specific characters are mentioned often, especially the main character. You won't see nearly as much of that when looking at *Destroyer*'s reviews. Those reviews talk about the story as a whole, or a specific bit of action the readers like. My audience has some overlap with Lindsay's, but there are differences— differences you need to train yourself to spot.

Only you can determine what your book is like, and which author's fans are most likely to pick it up. This is something that you might get wrong, especially the first couple of times you try it. Be patient, and keep learning. Every time you launch a book, you have another chance to zero in on the right audience.

My first novel didn't make me a six-figure author. Publishing over and over until I learned the ropes did.

**Exercise #4-** Go to Amazon and pick two genres you

think your book fits into. Ex: For my *Deathless* series, those genres are SF and Mystery/Thriller. Browse the top 100 for your two categories, with an eye for any book you think might be similar to yours. Read the blurbs, look at the covers. Once you've found one you think might be close to yours, purchase that book.

Normally this part would be a bonus, but since it's so vital I'm making it part of the regular exercise. *Read the damned book.* I know we're distracted by Netflix, social media, and a host of real world obligations. Carve out 20-30 minutes a day to just read. Do it daily, until you finish the book you selected.

**Bonus:** Pick a second and third book, and read those, too.

## 6

## SERIAL READERS

The holy grail of audiences is the serial readers of the world. If you can attract a small tribe of them, you will supercharge your career. Let me repeat that: you don't need a ton of them. Just a handful is often enough to kickstart Amazon's quest to sell your book. Remember that Amazon is looking for people who exactly match those people who bought it.

If a couple hundred serial readers buy your book, then Amazon has enough to work with. Now they can start showing the book to other serial readers. If those readers like it, they'll buy it. That will start the snowball effect. That's why it's so important to understand not just serial readers, but those serial readers who love *your* genre. Finding them begins with understanding both them and their needs.

That's easier if you are or used to be a serial reader yourself. I was while growing up, and I know many of you were as well.

Serial readers are easy to identify. They always have a small stack of books (or ebooks), which they plow through like other people plow through shows on Netflix. They binge-read, often devouring a full novel every day. They love series, because a series allows them to stay in the same universe for weeks, or for epic series occasionally months (I'm looking at you, *Wheel of Time*).

It may feel like our world is too distracted for such people to exist, and it's true that the number of serial readers has dwindled slightly with the advent of so many competing entertainment options. But the world is a big place. There are **tens of millions of serial readers**, spanning the entire globe. People in Russia, Australia, India, and Canada are all buying the same books.

Economy of scale is incredibly powerful. We can tap into serial readers across the globe, but in order to do that we need to understand those readers. Why do people devour a book a day? If you want to become a six-figure author, you need to know the answer for *your* target audience. So let's learn how to do that.

**Reader Psychology**

The original title for this book was *Reader Psychology*. I considered the topic important enough to warrant a book, but I eventually realized no one would buy a book with that title. Understanding what it is and why it matters is, in my opinion, the most valuable takeaway from this entire book. It isn't sexy, but it *is* powerful.

So what is it? Reader psychology is exactly what it sounds like: the psychology of why people read. What do they get out of it? What makes them pick up a book at all, and why science fiction or romance over, say, something like a western?

The answers begin with *you*. Presumably, you like to read. Almost every author I know does, and most of us read a lot as children. I used to devour a fantasy novel a day, and would reread books if I ran out. It was all I wanted to do, which made me the ideal serial reader.

Tapping into ten-year-old Chris isn't that hard. I vividly remember picking up my first *Dragonlance* novel. A bearded half-elf ranger stood protectively next to a knight and a beautiful priestess. Behind them, a menacing red dragon curled around the top of a mountain. What more could you ask for?

Forty-year-old me can look analytically at why my younger self was so enthralled. My love of fantasy began at the age of seven when my brother and I were dropped off at the Scottsdale Public Library on a random Saturday. They were playing a cartoon with a projector. It was called *The Hobbit*. After the movie, I couldn't shut up about it, and my father told me that it was based on a book.

I rushed to the fantasy section and checked out *The Hobbit*. It was even better than the movie, so I looked for other books. I found *The Chronicles of Prydain*. I found Narnia. These worlds were amazing, and I loved them. They were undiscovered places where anything was possible, where a kid like me could be special.

As I grew older, the pattern continued. I read books every day, always searching for new worlds to explore. That exploration, that relentless curiosity to delve into the unknown, was what drove me. I loved comic books, and TV shows like *Star Trek*, *Buffy*, *Firefly*, *Lost*, and *Battlestar Galactica*. Every last one shared that same theme: a new frontier, pregnant with the undiscovered.

It turns out there are millions of other readers

with stories very similar to mine, people who grew up with the same books, movies, and television shows. Interestingly, these people span every age group. A sixteen-year-old and an eighty-three-year-old both wrote to me in the same week to tell me they loved the *Firefly* reference in one of my books.

This intrigued me, so I emailed one of my lists to ask them why they read. Most people wrote back with detailed stories of how they discovered a genre at a young age, and how it had shaped their lives. A few made the discovery later in life, but are just as eager as their younger counterparts. What's interesting is that both groups used some of the same words in their responses. Words like:

- Discovered
- New (universes, magic, places, frontiers)
- Powers, Magic

A few dozen readers is hardly a scientific study, but it definitely suggests something important: the people who read my genre seem to share the same driving needs. Those needs may shift dramatically for *your* serial readers, depending on genre. That's both good and bad news. Good news, because it means that somewhere in the world serial readers exist for whatever you write. Bad news, because I can't just give you a list. You need to discover the needs of your own audience.

I can at least tell you how I went about doing that. When I dug a little deeper into my own childhood reading, I realized that watching heroes grow to overcome challenges was something I craved. I wanted to see good guys overcome insurmountable odds, learning about themselves and their friends as they did so. I wanted to live vicariously through fiction, safe in a secret world no one in my ordinary life knew or understood.

As I got older, I needed more and more sophisticated books to fill that need, but the underlying needs didn't change. The books I most loved at age ten are exactly the same thing I love to read today. Instead of *Lord of the Rings*, I'm reading *The Stormlight Archives*.

This is why I recommend so strongly in *Write to Market* that you write what you love. Your stories are the product of every other story you've read, watched, or acted out through your entire life. Write what you love, because somewhere out there lies a tribe of geeks who love the same thing. They read and watched all the same stuff, and loved it just as much as you did. Finding them is so much easier if you're already one of them. You can use yourself as a template.

Where would seventeen-year-old you hang out if she were devouring urban fantasy books the way you did? What social media would she use? If she went to Amazon today, what books would she pick up? Would she talk about them on Tumblr? Or Reddit?

Remember that there are millions of variations of you in the world, people with similar experiences, and/or similar likes. There are millions who read romance. Millions more who love mysteries, or thrillers. Find your tribe. It's out there, trust me.

**Exercise #5-** How many books have you read in the last year? Are you a serial reader? If the answer is no, was there ever a time in your life when you were? What books did/do you read, and what do you love about them? Pick your favorite book, and make a bulleted list with everything you can think of that makes it your favorite. Looking at your list, what needs is that book filling for you?

**Bonus:** If you were a serial reader who just discovered whatever book you used in the exercise, where would you hang out to discuss it? How might you have discovered that book? If you're unsure, do a Google search for the book. Do you see it on Facebook? Tumblr? Instagram? Twitter? Goodreads? Find at least one place where current serial readers like to discuss the book. If the book you chose is old enough that you can't find much, see if you can pick a more recent favorite book.

## 7

## JOINING YOUR TRIBE

I n the last chapter you did some of the legwork to identify your serial reader. Here's where that research pays off. Serial readers rave about the things they love, and often do it in very social communities. These can be forums, Facebook groups, or even YouTube comments.

If you want to become a six-figure author, you need to discover the communities where your serial readers hang out. That's time-consuming work, but it's something I enjoy a great deal. Why? Because it means I get to hang out with a bunch of fellow science fiction & fantasy geeks. We talk about the things that I love, everything from current shows we watch to—wait for it—our favorite new books.

By being a part of these communities, I am exposed to the current crop of new content in my favorite genre. People often recommend books, movies, shows, music, or even video games. By playing/watching/reading these, I put my finger on the pulse of my target audience. I get to see how they react to the latest *Game of Thrones*. I can see where George broke reader expectations, and where he met them.

I get to see what people loved about these stories, and what they hated. This provides an amazing degree of context when writing your books, and when trying to find the people who will love the ones you've already written.That's a huge advantage over every author who just writes their novels in a complete vacuum.

In the last chapter, the bonus part of the exercise asked you to figure out where your serial reader hangs out. This isn't an exact science, but a quick Google search should give you some starting points. There are Facebook groups devoted to every topic imaginable. There are large social media aggregate sites like Reddit or Tumblr. There's Twitter, or Goodreads.

Obviously you aren't going to be able to master them all, nor should you try. What you want is one or two places where your readers hang out. The easiest way to dip a toe in is to start with just one.

You find someplace that looks interesting, and you lurk quietly. Do people here talk about books? How often? If it seems like a place where people do, then jump to the Etiquette section of this chapter. If not, keep looking until you find a place where people *do* discuss the books your target serial readers love. They're out there somewhere.

## Etiquette

Almost all of us have been that guy or girl. We've shown up in a new community, and embarrassed the hell out of ourselves—OMGIhavethisbookandyoushouldbuyit—all in a rush, before we've even really introduced ourselves. You simply cannot do that, or the community will blacklist you. When you find this community, you should first lurk for a few days while you read threads and see how people interact.

When you have something relevant to add to the conversation, you chime in. That's it, unless there's a place the community will allow you to introduce yourself. If they do, it's okay to mention in that thread that you're an author. Once. You don't get to tell them about your books, or mention your upcoming release.

Instead, your job is to post about the stuff the community is interested in. What did you think of the *Walking Dead* season opener? Join the conversation, and when you feel comfortable, start creating your own threads. These threads need to be topical; again, you aren't allowed to post about your book.

Why? Because you need to build trust, and this cannot be faked. If you're there with an agenda, the community will sense it. Worse, you won't enjoy posting there because you aren't truly interested in the topics these people are discussing. You're there to sell books. That's a lose/lose situation, and you want to avoid it at all costs.

Instead, keep searching communities until you find one that clicks. Yes, this can be time consuming. Yes, it could take weeks or even months to settle into a few relevant communities. That seems like a lot of work just to learn more about your audience, I get that. But putting in that work lays the foundation for your career.

The power of understanding my target audience is instrumental to my success. You can duplicate or exceed it, but only if you go about this with deliberate care. Cultivate your audience slowly. Learn from them. Be courteous, and for the love of God don't be that guy or girl who is constantly spamming about their book.

These people will spot your humblebrag a mile away. Don't do it.

## What If You Don't Have Time?

What if you simply don't have the time to become an active part of your target audience? If you want to make a lucrative living doing this, then I suggest you find the time. That often requires sacrifices, but those sacrifices are worth it.

I used to be very active on all sorts of writer forums, but these days I invest that time on Reddit and other similar communities. I do that because I want to be part of the tribe I write for. I want to understand my target audience, and that requires me to be a part of that audience. You will never truly understand them until you become them.

Much of the time I previously devoted to online communities like Kboards is now spent BSing about which cylon was the biggest reveal. Or what might happen in the next season of *Game of Thrones*. Or a host of less recognizable things that my target audience loves to talk about.

I made that time, and it came at a cost. Do I miss checking in at Kboards several times a day? Sure. I love meeting other authors, and I've learned some great things there. But that community will never help me understand my target audience. Worse, I allowed it to become a time suck. I'd spend hours a day posting.

*Did the KU payout drop this month?* or *You'll never believe what this author did!* Threads like these consumed a disproportionate amount of my time, time that I've now invested in my tribe. I have street credit in the communities I joined, because I spend a fair amount of time there. The cost was steep, but I remain convinced that this is the right path.

Don't get me wrong. I still post in a few author communities, but I do it much less than I used to. That time is valuable, and the best long-term career move I can make is spending it with my target audience.

## What If I'm an Introvert?

This is by far the most difficult barrier I've had to

overcome to get where I am. A party, for me, is seven people. I don't like leaving the house, and neither does my wife. We're hermits, and we love it. Flying somewhere like Austin, Texas for the Smarter Artist Summit took enormous willpower. I knew I was going to do a lot of extroverting, and any introvert reading this understands the cost that carries.

I know how difficult it is to interact, and I know all about social anxiety. Unfortunately, if you want to reach the lofty heights of six-figure authordom, you'll need to extrovert at least a little. It's difficult, but it gets easier with practice. When you find a prospective community, become a lurker. Don't post anything until you're comfortable doing so. When you are, start by adding comments to threads in the communities you've joined. Eventually, you can work up to posting your own thread.

These posts should be about things you are genuinely interested in. You don't need to (and shouldn't) post "buy my book" or anything about your books. Instead, talk about how awesome you think Tyrion is, and isn't it cool when Jon Snow did that thing. Be a real part of the community. That removes a lot of the social pressure, especially after you get to know those people.

If you post in communities like the Writer's Cafe

you already understand what gradually assimilating into one of these communities is like. It can become like a family if you let it, a family that loves all the same things you happen to write about.

**Exercise #6-** You already know what I'm going to say, don't you? You need to get out there and find the communities where your target reader hangs out. Run a Google search for "[YOUR TARGET BOOK] Facebook groups." Try another search for "[YOUR TARGET BOOK] forums." See what comes up. Do any of these places look like somewhere you'd enjoy hanging out?

**Bonus:** Brainstorm your own searches. Find a half dozen potential communities where your readers might live. Investigate each community, then select two or three to join.

## 8

## NETWORKING WITH AUTHORS

E arlier in the book, you did some research to find authors similar to you. Now it's time to reach out to those authors. You're doing this for several reasons, but the most important is that these people face the same challenges you do. They want to find the same readers you do. They want to be (and many already are) six-figure authors, just like you do. As indies, we're in this together, and some of the best guidance you ever receive will likely come from more experienced authors in your genre.

If you're a brand new author you don't know these people yet, and the idea of approaching a successful author might feel strange. Cold emailing someone is weird, right? Not really. I get at least a dozen of those emails a day, and triple that if I've recently done a podcast. Tons of people reach out, and many have become friends.

Let me be very clear though: you must not have an agenda when approaching someone. If you're trying to get something out of that author, they're going to figure it out. When they do, you can bet they're going to distance themselves. You must be genuine. Trust me when I say that's in your best interest anyway.

Having a larger author share your book to their list is great, but you can't go in with that as a goal. Instead, try to make friends with an author who writes the same stuff you do—an author that probably shares a whole bunch of your hobbies, or why else would they happen to write in the same genre?

When I was writing the *Void Wraith* trilogy, I often compared notes with a guy by the name of Richard Fox. He also writes Military SF, and he'd been doing it for a lot longer. Richard has given me timely advice about what his readers like, and given me several tips about marketing on Amazon. After we'd been doing this for a while, Richard announced *Destroyer* to his list. I returned the favor for *The Ember War*.

Both of us had actually read the books we were recommending, and I only did it because I genuinely loved *The Ember War*. We helped each other because we were friends, and because we both know we're in this together.

If I'd had an agenda when I met Richard, things might have gone very differently. My aim wasn't to get him to email his list. I was just happy to have an experienced SF author to point out the potholes I was about to step in. Instead, I ended up gaining a friend I'll likely know for years.

There is another benefit of networking with authors, though, one that will help propel you toward being a six-figure author.

## Multi-Author Box Sets

One of the best networking options available to indies is the multi-author box set. A group of authors will get together, each contributing their first-in-series novel. That box set can contain between five and twenty-five novels, depending on the organizers. The book will be released for 99 cents, making it a complete no-brainer for any serial reader who sees it.

It's easy for the authors involved to make sure a lot of readers do see it, because all of us let our respective lists know. Since we all write in the same genre, we're effectively cross-pollinating our audiences. Not just our mailing lists, but the customer profiles Amazon is using to market our work. The box set links our books together in Amazon's artificial brain.

I've been in several box sets thus far, and each is another pool of readers I'm slowly drawing in. I don't see an avalanche of sales, but I do see steady growth in both mailing list subscribers and reviews. The best part? Unless you're the person organizing the set, you as the author have to do almost no work.

If you're a small author and don't have the clout to get invited to such a set, you always have the option of starting your own. No one really wants to do the work involved, trust me on that. If you are, you'll usually be able to find authors in your genre willing to participate. If you can get one or two big names to serve as a sort of anchor, then you can add a series of small and medium-sized authors to round out your box.

As a word of caution: if you're going to go this route make sure that you understand the terms of whatever agreement you reach. Will the set stay in KU, and if so for how long? How will all authors be paid? How long will the book stay 99 cents, and what will the long-term price be? Hammer those things out, and box sets can be a godsend.

Also consider anthologies, which are similar but different enough to warrant a quick mention. In an anthology, each author is contributing a unique short story that probably hasn't appeared anywhere else. This requires more work from each author, but offers new content that everyone's fans may be interested in. This fills a very similar role: exposure to every author's audience.

**Exercise #7**- Pick three of the authors whose books you have actually read, and send them a message introducing yourself. This can be on Facebook, through email, or whatever other platform that author uses. Ask for nothing. You're just telling them that you exist, and what you liked about their book.

**Bonus:** Write a blog post review about one of the books you read. Tweet or share the review with the author.

## 9

## MASTERING MAILING LISTS

You now know that if you can funnel a few hundred serial readers to Amazon, you'll effectively train them to sell your book. You have some idea how to locate those people, though odds are good you haven't yet done much with that information.

Once you've gotten comfortable in the communities you've joined, you can finally explain to people that you're an author. Start by asking them if they'd like to join your advance review team. All they need to do is sign up to your mailing list, and they'll get a free book introducing them to your work.

If you've done your work well, every last person who signs up will be one of the serial readers you're after. Why? Because serial readers quickly run out of stuff to read. There just aren't enough new books being released, so they're the most willing to give up an email address to get more.

What if a few weeks before you released your next series you asked for ARC readers on the three largest communities you were a part of? What if fifty people signed up, and half those people went on to buy the book because they liked it?

Your long term success is tied to the lists you build. Fifty readers will become five hundred, then five thousand. The larger that number grows, the more power every release will have. That kind of momentum can very quickly lead to six figures.

## Mailing Lists

One of the most common pieces of advice you'll hear as an indie author is to start a mailing list. I even have a chapter about them in *Launch to Market*. After reading the book, a lot of newer authors email me to complain. They're tired of hearing it. They've started a list, but that list is growing too slowly, and it doesn't sell any books when they use it. So why do I keep harping on them?

The fact that your list isn't working doesn't mean mailing lists don't work. It just means you need to approach your mailing list differently. In order to use a mailing list, we need to understand both how to use it and how to grow it.

When I first started as an author, I followed the prevailing wisdom and made my mailing list. Like many of you, I had no idea how to use it or how to get people to sign up. I was mystified. I mean, I knew I needed to let the list know about my books as I released them. But what else? I was lost, and don't mind admitting it.

Thankfully, I invested the time in learning more about how mailing lists are used. I talked to successful authors about how they were doing it. I talked to people in internet marketing, a much more mature industry. In the end, I learned enough to build and use my lists with confidence.

Today, I have seven different mailing lists, and my number of lists has ranged as high as ten depending on which temporary lists I've created. If you total up all my subscribers I have just shy of 5,500, but my biggest list is a little over 2,000 people. Why do I segregate them like that? Purity of data.

People who are interested in my *Deathless* series don't care about my *Void Wraith* trilogy, and vice versa. They're two distinctly different groups of fans, and I approach them very differently. I would never send the same email to both groups. I personalize my emails to fit the list. My lists for writers don't mind hearing about fiction releases, but if I'm going to tell them, I have to make it relevant for them. I'll often break down my launch statistics, which is helpful to other writers. It's vital that you speak to each audience in a way that fits them.

Far more importantly, segregating my lists into relevant audiences allows me to use them to train Amazon and Facebook. When a book for writers comes out, I'll alert about 1,500 people on my lists. The other 4,000 will never hear about it, but that's by design. Could I sell a few more books if I told everybody? Absolutely. But having writers buy your novel isn't helping you.

The immediate income might be nice, but the cost is staggering. Using my lists incorrectly will confuse the heck out of Amazon. So I'm very selective in how I use them. My lists are my most valuable asset outside of the books themselves. Our entire careers are predicated upon enough people knowing about our books to pay us a sustainable income. Lists are that important.

## Getting People on Your List

The simplest and most effective way to get mailing list subscribers is to showcase your list in the front and back matter of your novel. Every time someone downloads your book it will be the first and last thing they see. It's something you can set up once, and then it just runs for the life of your series. People will always trickle in to that list.

This advice is explained at length in Nick Stephenson's book *Reader Magnets*, so I won't belabor it here. It works. The book is a free download, and it's still just as relevant as the day it was written. The rest of this section assumes that you know what a reader magnet is, so if it's unclear, please give Nick's book a look.

What I *will* get into is the most effective way to get people to sign up via the front and back matter. The best way to do that is, of course, a reader magnet. Give them something for free in exchange for their email address. I've seen authors use short stories, character sheets, and artwork to incentivize people to join their list. I've experimented with most of those myself.

What did I learn? Not all reader magnets are created equal. When I launched my *Deathless* series I quickly cranked out a short story called *The First Ark*. It was set 12,000 years ago, the backstory of an

Egyptian goddess. The series itself took place in modern day. After I started offering *The First Ark* as an incentive to sign up to my list, signups tripled.

Still, I had this nagging feeling that I'd missed an opportunity. When I launched *Destroyer*, I was determined to make better use of my reader magnet. This time around, I decided to write something readers would be far more interested in. In *Destroyer* we learn that Commander Nolan has been exiled to the $14^{th}$ fleet, but we don't know exactly why. It has something to do with an admiral's daughter, but it isn't ever directly addressed in the novel.

My reader magnet was called *Exiled*, and it answered that question. It was about 12,000 words long, and gave the direct backstory for the protagonist. One in five people who bought *Destroyer* signed up to the mailing list. **93% of those people downloaded Exiled**. I had over a thousand signups the first month.

Then I made the mistake of listing *Exiled* on Amazon. The instant people could buy it for 99 cents, mailing list signups tanked. To date, *Exiled* has made about $3,000. You know what? If I had it to do over I'd never have listed it on Amazon, and going forward my reader magnets will always be exclusive to people who sign up to my list.

If you give readers the answer to a question they really want answered, and you require them to join your list to get the answer, then most of them will do exactly that. Try it.

**Sales Lead to Signups**

There are all sorts of ways to get people on your list. You can run Facebook ads. You can post on Reddit, or Twitter. All of those methods pale in comparison to sales. The fastest way to grow your list is to sell a lot of books. If you're using an effective reader magnet, a first book in a new series can quickly net hundreds of signups. If you're following the advice about finding serial readers, you have a much higher likelihood of getting the kind of sales that will grow your list.

The icing on the cake is that these signups will be engaged readers. These are people who love your stuff, and many will be the very serial readers you most want to reach. These people will respond when you email, they'll buy your next book, and will ensure that Amazon has been properly trained to sell that book.

If you have no sales, you will have very few

signups. That's a tough hill to climb, and my advice may be tough to hear. You may need to write the first book in a new series if your existing series has flatlined. The launch of a book is the single best window to generate sales, which also makes it the very best window to grow your mailing list. Use that sixty day window wisely.

That said, if your series has languished, that doesn't mean it can't be resurrected. That can be done with effective advertising, which we'll discuss in the next chapter.

### How Often Should I Email My List?

Once you have a list, what the heck do you do with it? How often should you pester people?

Different lists have an entirely different set of rules. I sent an email every day for 21 days when I did the 21 Day Novel Writing Challenge (those videos are are still up), and I only had two unsubscribes the entire time. If I'd sent that many emails to any other list, *everyone* would have unsubscribed. Those lists would be wastelands.

You should contact each list as often as you can provide content they will find valuable. For example, these days I send out a video once a week instead of every day. I have almost no unsubscribes, because the only time I ever email that list is when I've got a new video. I'm giving them something, not asking them to buy something.

The same is true for a fiction list. I only email them when one of my books comes out. I'll usually email them again a few weeks later when audio comes out. Other than that, the only time I've contacted my list was when the *Star Heroes* box set went live. I did that both because I knew it would result in sales and because I knew my list would enjoy getting seven novels for a dollar. Serial readers love deals.

That's it. I don't send newsletters about my life, because my readers don't care. Remember, though: that's just *my* readers. Some readers *will* care. Wayne Stinnett has incredible reader engagement, and he emails his list all the time. They know all about his life, which admittedly is pretty damned fascinating. (Shameless plug for his book for writers, *Blue Collar to No Collar*).

Experimentation is the only way to find out what works with your list. You can measure success based on the number of unsubscribes, versus the open/click-through rate. If only a handful unsubscribe, and a whole bunch click the links in your email, then that's a winner. If, on the other hand, you have a whole bunch of unsubscribes and very little engagement, you missed the mark.

That's totally okay. You're far better off emailing your list regularly and making some mistakes in the process. Don't make the mistake I did, and not email your list for several months at a time because you don't want to bother them. That results in a cold list. A cold list will forget who you are, and people will unsubscribe in droves whenever you contact them.

You're after the happy medium. Email your list when you have stuff they want to know about, and produce stuff they want to know about often enough that they don't forget about you.

### Ways I've Used My List

Hopefully you've got a general idea of how to use your list, but I thought it might be helpful to list some of the ways I've used mine. You can ask your lists all sorts of things, and many people will be happy to answer. Here are a few ways I've utilized lists:

- Polls for titles, cover art, or the next book you should write. Asking people what they want more of not only raises engagement, but I've ended up with great suggestions for titles or plot points I'd never have come up with on my own.

- Information on the audience. How did they discover your book? How many books do they read a month? This will teach you a lot about your specific audience, which will make it easier to tailor your emails. Readers love talking about this stuff, too.

- Do they have a favorite character? Or a favorite scene? What do they think is going to happen in the next book? This is one of my favorite methods, because it lets me talk directly with readers. I've made friends that way, not to mention superfans.

- I asked my writers lists whether or not I should do a high-priced course. The response convinced me I shouldn't, saving me a lot of time and energy better spent writing more books.

**Exercise #8-** This one looks short, but may take more work than any other exercise. Set up a brand new mailing list with a mailing provider like Mailchimp. You want a new list, because you're going to populate that list with your target readers. You don't want it polluted from any existing signups.

Once you've got your list, brainstorm an effective reader magnet to offer that list. Can you tie something into your main narrative? What characters do fans want to know more about?

**Bonus:** Take a few days off from your work in progress, and blast out your reader magnet. Get it done, and start giving it away.

## 10

# EFFECTIVE ADVERTISING

Advertising scares the hell out of authors. Most of us have lost money on ads, from Facebook to Amazon to book promotion services. We spend money, and we don't sell books. It's frustrating, costly, and feels like we're spinning our tires in the mud. This is especially true when we first start experimenting.

The reality is that advertising is a skill, just like writing. It's an expensive skill to master, even if you're being as frugal as possible. Here's the thing: Mastering advertising is one of the most important things you can do to become a six-figure author. You need to learn how to create a steady stream of both sales and email signups. Doing that is what will secure your career over the long term.

Advertising is an amazing way of getting new

eyes on your books. I've had literally millions of impressions on the *Void Wraith* trilogy. Most of those impressions cost me nothing, just the few thousand that resulted in clicks. I've lost a little money on those clicks, but only in the short term.

Hear me out.

*Destroyer* retails for $2.99. My pay-per click varies from platform to platform, but on average I get enough sales to cover 90% of the cost of the advertising. I pay a dollar, and I get back ninety cents. That sounds like a losing proposition, until you consider two things.

Eighty percent of the people who buy *Destroyer* go on to buy *Void Wraith*. Ninety percent of those people go on to buy *Eradication*. My sell-through means that while a sale costs me about $3, I earn about $7.70. That means that the advertising works out to be profitable, because I have an entire trilogy. The longer my series, the more acceptable a loss on advertising for book one is.

The other, far more important, reason to advertise is the mailing list signups. About 10% of the people who buy *Destroyer* sign up to the list. That means every day I'm getting more subscribers, and every time I tell them about anything I make a little more money as a result. Someone I added today could spend $25 on various books over the course of the next year.

The final, ultimate reason to advertise is purity of data. If you use ten dollars a day on either Facebook or Amazon ads, you'll get a trickle of sales to the serial readers in your genre. But how do you go from *knowing* that advertising can work, to *making* it work?

You need to define your audience in a way that places like Amazon and Facebook can understand. This can mean making a list of relevant keywords, or finding interests (like military science fiction) that you can use for ads.

## Define Your Audience

Earlier in the book we explained how machine learning works. You need to feed Amazon data in the form of customers. Those customers need to be serial readers in your genre. You can learn about those people by hanging out at the same forums, or the same social media. Joining that tribe will teach you more about them, and what they like. That should include what books they like. Have you ever seen the Karate Kid? You've been waxing cars and painting fences.

Those books and authors are going to form the basis for the keywords you use in your advertising. You want as many authors and books in your genre as possible. I went so far as to research a number of bestseller lists on Goodreads. I added every author, their series, and their book titles to a list of keywords.

When I did Facebook advertising, I added as many of them as I was able to. Not every author or series can be used in advertising, but some could. Those were the ones I focused on. Some lost me money; on some, I broke even. A few have been profitable. I terminate the worst performing ones, and keep the ones that are performing.

Amazon ads are easier to target, since you can use a lot more specific keywords. Unfortunately, their reporting is terrible and can be delayed by as much as 48 hours. This makes it really easy to lose money, since you can't quickly adjust your ads like you can with Facebook. Both systems have pros and cons, and which you use is up to you. You can also experiment with Google AdWords, though I only know one author who's had any success doing so.

Regardless of the platform you choose, the goal

is the same: you want to learn which authors and books convince people to buy yours. Finding that answer can be costly, but once you know who you're most similar to it becomes much cheaper. My cost per click has dropped over time, because I'm always refining which keywords I use.

Those keywords are how you define your audience. Learn what they like, and pay close attention to your reviews. If you use "David Brin" as a keyword and it starts selling books, look to see if any of your new readers mention him. If you're a snoop like I am, click on the account for people who leave reviews and see what other reviews they've left. What books do they love? What books do they hate?

Many of my best keywords came from just that sort of experimentation. It takes work, time, and money...but wow, are the results worth it. Now my ads are close to break-even, and I'll be the first to admit that I haven't spent as much time as I should making them more profitable.

## Look-Alike Audiences

One of the most powerful things you can do with your mailing list is to create a look-alike audience.

Basically, you feed a list of email addresses to a company like Facebook, and they use machine learning to identify all the similarities between the people on your list. If your list is comprised entirely of serial readers, guess who Facebook is going to go out and find? More serial readers.

This kind of targeting is what gets you from taking a loss on ads to making a profit. It's only possible, though, if you have a highly targeted list. If your list isn't pure, then neither is your advertising. The better you do your job building the list, the more profit your ads will generate. A poorly targeted look-alike audience won't do squat, no matter how large it is.

This more than anything else is why I'm exclusive with Amazon right now. I've generated thousands of signups, and plan to add many thousands more. I'm already using these lists for my ads, and the difference in cost is amazing. Almost every profitable ad has a look-alike audience associated with it.

Even if I one day cut ties with Amazon, I can always use the lists I've built to train Facebook, Google, or other advertisers. Data is data, and if yours is good you'll be able to use it for the rest of your career.

## Launch Advertising

The conventional advice I see touted at Kboards is that you should do a book promotion centered around your launch. Most authors discount their book to 99 cents, and will often use book promotion sites to get the word out. That's exactly what I did with *No Such Thing As Werewolves*. I lost almost a thousand dollars, and had barely a hundred sales.

What if I'd invested that same money in Facebook or Amazon ads? I could have done a hundred dollars a day in advertising for the first week—and had I known back then what I do now, I could have targeted the right audience. Not only would I have lost less money (or maybe even made a profit), but each and every sale would have been to someone in my target audience. My list signups and also-bought books would have been perfectly targeted.

For my last two launches, all I've done is Facebook and Amazon ads to promote them. I save the book promotion sites for backlist books, because those books have already built up a list. I'm not so worried about polluting it with a few promotion sales.

**Exercise #9-** Use the research you've done in previous chapters to make a list of authors, series, and titles that you feel are applicable to your book. Once you have a list, create an Amazon ad using those keywords. Give the ad a low daily spend, so you aren't bankrupting yourself.

Let the ad run for one week, and see which keywords perform. Keep those going, and cut the rest. Continue this cycle, always adding more keywords while pruning dead ones.

## 11

## FEEDING THE BEAST

One of the ugly realities about being a six-figure author is that you're reliant on Amazon. Amazon changes quickly, and readers have short memories. If they're waiting a year in between books, readers will have long since forgotten you when you release your sequel. I made that mistake in my *Deathless* series, and I paid the price.

Your goal should be to release books no more than two months apart. If this isn't something you can easily do, it could be worth holding back the first couple books in a series until you have three or more. That can mean a big up-front investment, but wow, can it do wonders for your income.

I released *Destroyer* on March 28th, *Void Wraith* on June 6th, and *Eradication* on September 9th. That's two months to book two, and three months to book three. My worst month of the year was August, because it had been a full sixty days since I'd last released a book. Every month without a new release drops my income by about 30%.

Amazon has a voracious need for new content, and if we want a healthy six-figure income we need to feed that beast. This is doubly true for romance, which has an even shorter release window than science fiction. Readers want content, and they want it now. We need to get faster, and we need to write better books. That may sound like a tall order, but the single largest ingredient is practice. You get that every time you put out another book.

**The Cliffs of Despair**

If you spend any time in author communities you will eventually hear someone talk about the 30-day and 60-day cliffs. They're referring to the fact that Amazon does the most promotion for your book during the 30 days after its release, and that after 60 days they stop all the active promotion they give to new releases.

That's only part of the problem, though.

Amazon's machine learning has linked your book to all sorts of other books. Those other books also have a 30- and 60-day cliff; every time one of them falls off, it weakens your book, too. Every product on Amazon is slowly decaying in that way, and no amount of promotion is going to prolong that indefinitely.

The only way to stave off the cliffs of despair is more books. If you use preorders and release a book every sixty days, then you always have a book on Amazon's Hot New Release list. Their algorithms are always peddling your books, and they're linking them to the books in your genre that are hot *right now*.

That might seem impossible, but while you haven't yet achieved it, it doesn't mean you won't if you keep practicing.

**Exercise #10-** Take a good look at your production schedule for the next 12 months. How many books are you going to write? How quickly will they be released? Based on your writing speed, would it be worthwhile to delay releasing the first one so you can put out two at once? Once you have the answers, add completion dates to your calendar for the rough draft of the next three books.

## 12

## PERFECTING YOUR PROCESS

My first year as an author was a frenzy of blunders and cut corners, and I think that's true for most of us. To be a successful indie author you need to master business, writing, marketing, copywriting, and about a dozen other skills.

The way I've survived is by adopting the Pareto Principle. For those not familiar, that's the 80/20 rule. About 80% of your success comes from 20% of your actions. In the startup world, this meant releasing a minimum viable product. I'd create 80% of the app we really wanted, in the quickest, dirtiest caffeine-fueled month you can imagine.

We'd then see what our users liked and disliked. Some features we thought they'd love weren't used at all. Some we thought were minor turned out to be their favorites. Our customers taught us, but they could only do that because we'd actually released something for them to use.

The same is true for us as authors. No one will ever read your book until you publish it. Your first novel will be the hardest, because you'll know the least. Through publishing that first novel, you learn all sorts of things about craft and about marketing. This is true for every book you release. Each one will be a little different—and hopefully a little better— because you've been learning along the way.

Improving your processes is a huge quality of life change, and can mean selling a whole lot more books for a lot less effort. Below, I'm going to cover some of the processes I've streamlined over the last two years. Some will work for you, others may not be a good fit. The important takeaway isn't the specific processes I'm looking at. The takeaway is that examining your own processes is key to becoming a six-figure author. You can't afford to set it and forget it. You need to be improving, constantly.

If you master the holy trinity of writing, editing, and marketing, you will never work for anyone else again.

## Be a Better Writer

If you've read *5,000 Words Per Hour*, you know how I feel about tracking your writing. Tracking your daily word counts will do more to increase your productivity than almost anything else I can offer. Remember that what can be tracked can be improved. Track your writing, and over time take a careful look at what you're seeing.

Identify your most productive times, and see if you can figure out why they're the most productive. Do you write your book all in a three-week binge, or are you more comfortable with a steady, daily word count? Find the system that works for you, and always be looking for ways to improve that system.

Remember to work on craft, always. I read two craft books a month, and I practice the things they teach. The indie author space is already getting more crowded, and that will only accelerate over the next few years. If you want to make a living at this, you need to be a great author. That comes from constantly striving to improve both story and prose.

## Master the Editing Process

Mastering the editing process is tricky, especially for authors with more limited means. Editors can be expensive, and you often have no idea whether or not the person you're paying has any idea what they're doing. I've shelled out thousands of dollars to people totally unqualified to edit my books, and I paid the price for that in reviews.

This is another area where relying on other authors for guidance can be extremely helpful. Ask the authors in your genre who they use. Get a peek at their editing process. Are they using a line editor? A developmental editor? How many proofreaders, if any? You can use their editing process as a starting point to create your own. That process will change from book to book, but the goal is to make it better, cleaner, and cheaper over time.

In *Write to Market*, I talked about reducing my editing to just a quick line edit. I saved myself several thousand dollars per book, but the result was books laden with typos. Those books sell by the thousands, so the typos don't seem to prevent readers from buying. I've still resolved to release higher quality work. Why? Because the longer I do this, the easier it becomes to set up a process that will achieve cleaner books.

When I published *Destroyer* I had neither the

bandwidth nor time to work in additional editing. Now my editor and I have a fantastic system, and since we've worked on so many books together we're able to edit them far more quickly. These days I have Tammi do a line edit with some developmental suggestions. I implement her changes, then send the book to a proofreader I trust. That's it.

It's the happy medium between the process I originally used and the one I advocated in *Write to Market*. It's still fast, and still less expensive, but it's just enough to ensure that I'm putting out books I can be proud of.


## Be a Better Marketer

This is the hat most authors still feel unqualified to wear. Marketing is daunting, but it gets less so the more you do it. Once you understand that you're really just trying to figure out what your target reader wants, it becomes something you can get a handle on.

Don't get me wrong, there's a lot of work involved. You're going to have to read, study your peers, and become involved with the serial readers in your genre. Over time, that will all become second nature. Don't worry too much about it right now; just get started. Try something. Make a post. You'll occasionally screw up, but you know what? No one will remember that in a year.

In three years you could be a successful six-figure author. Do you think anyone will care that you screwed up the blurb for your second book? Action is always better than inaction. Try something, see if it works, then try something else. Keep trying to identify and reach your target readers, and keep building your lists.

Over time, your platform will grow. Keep learning, and adapting. Accept that this author career thing is a long-term investment. Neither Stephen King nor J.K. Rowling were household names at the start of their careers. It took a mixture of fortitude and faith to keep marketing themselves—in their cases to publishers, but in yours directly to your readers.

Write the books. Tell the right readers they exist. The rest is just a matter of time.

**Exercise #11**- Make a list of the top three mistakes you've made in publishing. Be brutally honest; only you will see this list. Spend a minute visualizing the mistake, and how it made you feel.

What did each mistake teach you? If you can sincerely say you've learned from it, then cross that mistake off the list. If you haven't learned enough to avoid one of them, keep that on the list and attach it to your monitor.

Every time you screw up monumentally, add it to the list. Every time you grow as an author from that mistake, cross it off. Over time you'll see the power of perfecting your process.

## 13

## MY FAVORITE CHAPTER

The last chapter of my books is always the most fun to write. This is my chance to open a direct dialogue with you, to offer encouragement and occasionally tough love.

Most of us were taught that authors don't make a ton of money, and that they have to suffer for their craft. Many of us subconsciously believe that we're selling out if we make a lot of money from our art, but the tortured artists criticizing commercial fiction make me want to stab myself in the eye with a pen. Who are we to judge?

Dan Brown's name is often said with scorn, but his books entertain millions. There is nothing unethical about selling a lot of books, or about wanting to make a great living telling stories. We don't have to apologize to anyone for writing quickly, writing often, and marketing well. Quite the oppo-site: many readers thank us for turning out so many entertaining stories.

Isaac Asimov had three typewriters, each with a different work in progress. He cranked out a few stories a week, and often squeezed in a novel-length piece too. That's right—he would often finish a novel in a week. Asimov produced over 7.5 million words across five hundred published works.

Do you think his favorite, or his best, piece of work was one of the first twenty? Or did cranking out millions of words improve Asimov as an author, allowing him to write better and better stories as his career went on?

The vast majority of us are at the beginning of our careers. The work we're producing now isn't nearly as good as what we'll one day produce, assuming we treat writing like a career. *5,000 Words Per Hour* was the first book for authors I put out. I've written 89% of the days in the year and a half since. I know that because I've tracked my writing. I've watched myself improve.

My first novel came out in October of 2014. My eighth novel came out in September of 2016. After every book, I spent a lot of time reflecting on what worked and what didn't, but I *never stopped writing*.

The books pay the rent. The skills we develop are ours for life.

It may feel like you're not making any progress as an author right now. It may feel like everything you've tried has failed, and that you'll never get there. If you try to do this alone, you may end up being right. So don't do it alone. Find other authors, both bigger and smaller than yourself. Learn from them. Teach them. Befriend them.

About a year and a half ago, an author friend was at her wits' end. She was in a tough financial spot, and a burst line filled her basement with raw sewage. She didn't have the money to have the problem taken care of. Another friend tattled to the writers' group we were all a part of. Thirty-five authors came together to help. We sent our friend $400 through PayPal, and she got the problem fixed.

At the time, this friend only had one book out, a haunting, bittersweet love story. She might be the most talented author I know, but she couldn't sell that book to save her life. Today that same author is making a comfortable six figures, and employing most of her family using her author business.

If you're not where you want to be as an author, give it time. Find a support system. Get to know other writers. Give of yourself. Help out any time you think you can. The relationships you build will support you through the lean times, and when that tide starts to rise you can celebrate as all the author boats are lifted.

Until then, come at this career with dogged persistence. No matter what happens, keep writing and keep publishing. The stories in you will be lost if you don't tell them, and if you tell them well enough you won't ever need to answer to an employer again.

Most people who've read this book won't become six-figure authors. Are you "most people"? Only you can decide.

-Chris

## EXERCISES

**Exercise #1**- Fire up Amazon's home page. Mouse over your account button and click on "Your Recommendations." You'll see a bunch of categories, each showing what Amazon thinks you're interested in.

Now run five searches for books in a genre you don't normally read. If nothing leaps to mind, just look up "Chris Fox." Click each of the books you searched for.

Go back to Your Recommendations. If the books you searched for were in a new category, it should now appear. In my case, I searched for Western Novels and clicked the first five books in the search. All of a sudden, Historical Books showed up in my recommendations. Creepy, right? That's the power of data science.

**Bonus**- Go to iTunes, Barnes & Noble, or Google Play. Repeat this exercise. Note that nothing visible changes. Only Amazon is reacting to immediate changes in data. The rest of the retailers are light years behind.

~

**Exercise #2-** This exercise won't teach you to sell books, but it will show you a simple, practical application for data science. Copy a chapter from your latest work in progress, then go to Wordclouds.com. Click the file button, which will open a menu. Select paste, and paste in the chapter you copied.

Look at the resulting word cloud. Notice that words that appear frequently are larger. I use this technique to identify words that I tend to over use. Never again will I use *acrid* 23 times in a single novel.

**Bonus:** Use this process for your entire novel, and eliminate any words you see yourself overusing.

~

**Exercise #3-** How long have you had your Amazon

account? Go to your purchase history, all the way back to the beginning...as far as it will let you. What was the first thing you bought? What are all the things you've bought since then? Spend a little time browsing. What do you think these things say about you to Amazon? How is Amazon using that data?

**Bonus:** Pick two years: the first year you had your Amazon account, and this year. How many books did you buy in each year? Has it gone up or down?

**Exercise #4-** Go to Amazon and pick two genres you think your book fits into. Ex: For my *Deathless* series, those genres are SF and Mystery/Thriller. Browse the top 100 for your two categories, with an eye for any book you think might be similar to yours. Read the blurbs, look at the covers. Once you've found one you think might be close to yours, purchase that book.

Normally this part would be a bonus, but since it's so vital I'm making it part of the regular exercise. *Read the damned book*. I know we're distracted by Netflix, social media, and a host of real world obligations. Carve out 20-30 minutes a day to just read. Do it daily, until you finish the book you selected.

**Bonus:** Pick a second and third book, and read those, too.

**Exercise #5-** How many books have you read in the last year? Are you a serial reader? If the answer is no, was there ever a time in your life when you were? What books did/do you read, and what do you love about them? Pick your favorite book, and make a bulleted list with everything you can think of that makes it your favorite. Looking at your list, what needs is that book filling for you?

**Bonus:** If you were a serial reader who just discovered whatever book you used in the exercise, where would you hang out to discuss it? How might you have discovered that book? If you're unsure, do a Google search for the book. Do you see it on Facebook? Tumblr? Instagram? Twitter? Goodreads? Find at least one place where current serial readers like to discuss the book. If the book you chose is old enough that you can't find much, see if you can find something more recent to use.

**Exercise #6-** You already know what I'm going to say, don't you? You need to get out there and find the communities where your target reader hangs out. Run a Google search for "[YOUR TARGET BOOK] Facebook groups." Try another search for "[YOUR TARGET BOOK] forums." See what comes up. Do any of these places look like somewhere you'd enjoy hanging out?

**Bonus:** Brainstorm your own searches. Find a half dozen potential communities where your readers might live. Investigate each community, then select two or three to join.

**Exercise #7-** Pick three of the authors whose books

you have actually read, and send them a message introducing yourself. This can be on Facebook, through email, or whatever other platform that author uses. Ask for nothing. You're just telling them that you exist, and what you liked about their book.

**Bonus:** Write a blog post review about one of the books you read. Tweet or share the review with the author.

**Exercise #8**- This one looks short, but may take more work than any other exercise. Set up a brand new mailing list with a mailing provider like Mailchimp. You want a new list, because you're going to populate that list with your target readers. You don't want it polluted from any existing signups.

Once you've got your list, brainstorm an effective reader magnet to offer that list. Can you tie something into your main narrative? What characters do fans want to know more about?

**Bonus:** Take a few days off from your work in

progress, and blast out your reader magnet. Get it done, and start giving it away.

**Exercise #9-** Use the research you've done in previous chapters to make a list of authors, series, and titles that you feel are applicable to your book. Once you have a list, create an Amazon ad using those keywords. Give the ad a low daily spend, so you aren't bankrupting yourself.

Let the ad run for one week, and see which keywords perform. Keep those going, and cut the rest. Continue this cycle, always adding more keywords while pruning dead ones.

**Exercise #10-** Take a good look at your production schedule for the next 12 months. How many books are you going to write? How quickly will they be released? Based on your writing speed, would it be worthwhile to delay releasing the first one so you can put out two at once? Once you have the answers, add completion dates to your calendar for the rough draft of the next three books.

**Exercise #11-** Make a list of the top three mistakes you've made in publishing. Be brutally honest; only you will see this list. Spend a minute visualizing the mistake, and how it made you feel.

What did each mistake teach you? If you can sincerely say you've learned from it, then cross that mistake off the list. If you haven't learned enough to avoid one of them, keep that on the list and attach it to your monitor.

Every time you screw up monumentally, add it to the list. Every time you grow as an author from that mistake, cross it off. Over time you'll see the power of perfecting your process.

Printed in Great Britain
by Amazon

77676435R00068